For Leslie, Steve + boys.

Hope this will give you the impetus to see our part of the continent!

Doris + Julian
1996

D0597679

CARLA SOFFRITTI

FROM THE WOODLANDS TO THE OCEAN

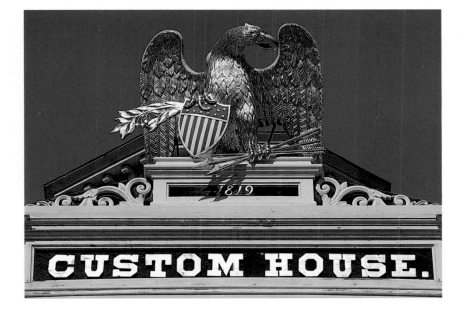

N E W   E N G L A N D

CONTENTS

Text
Carla Soffritti

Graphic design
Patrizia Balocco

Editorial coordination
Valeria Manferto De Fabianis
Laura Accomazzo
Alberto Bertolazzi

Maps
Cristina Franco

Translation
Ann Hylands Ghiringhelli

The Publisher would like to
thank the Office of Travel and
Tourism the Commonwealth
of Massachussets

© 1996 White Star S.r.l.
Via Candido Sassone, 22/24
13100 Vercelli, Italy.

All rights reserved. No part of this publication
may be reproduced, stored in a retrieval system
or transmitted in any form by any means
electronic, mechanical, photocopying
or otherwise, without first obtaining written
permission of the copyright owner.

This edition published in 1996
by Smithmark Publishers,
a division of U.S. Media Holdings,
Inc., 16 East 32nd Street, New York,
NY 10016.

SMITHMARK books are available for
bulk purchase, for sales promotion
and premium use. For details write or
call the manager of special sales,
SMITHMARK Publishers, 16 East
32nd Street, New York, NY 10016;
(212) 532-6600.

Produced by: White Star S.r.l.
Via Candido Sassone, 22/24
13100 Vercelli, Italy.

ISBN: 0-8317-4228-3

Printed in 1996
by Grafedit, Bergamo, Italy.

1 About thirty kilometres north of Boston, in Massachusetts, is the town of Salem, also known as "Witch City" after a still amply commemorated event of three centuries ago: a witchhunt conducted with frightening zeal. In the 18th century Salem was also a flourishing seaport from which ships sailed to far-away destinations, and the wealthiest trading centre of the USA; this less-known side of its history is revealed to present-day visitors to the Custom House.

2-3 Fronting the Atlantic Ocean, Newport (Rhode Island) is a smart tourist port, renowned for sailing events that on occasions fill the sports (and society) pages of newspapers the world over. For many years its harbour hosted the America's Cup, the most prestigious international regatta.

4-5 Overlooking the harbour and the waters of the Atlantic are some of Boston's finest waterfront buildings. For centuries harbour and ocean were the lifeblood of the city. In bygone days great merchant ships carrying goods to and from the Far East set sail from here; today it is the terminus of the "water shuttle", connecting the capital of Massachusetts with Logan Airport. Boston is unofficially considered the capital of New England, an area which extends from north of New York to east of the Hudson River valley.

6-7 In the villages of Vermont everything is ready for Halloween (October 31), the night when witches, spirits and other spooky creatures come out of hiding. To avoid being tormented by their pranks, wear a disguise and hang a pumpkin outside your front-door.

8 In the Berkshires, on the far western side of Massachusetts, Pittsfield is a town of decorous, dignified houses. Just outside the town is Arrowhead, the farm where Herman Melville wrote his celebrated "Moby Dick". It was during the last century that this region first became an enclave popular with great numbers of rich New Yorkers and Bostonians. Other famous past residents include novelist Nathaniel Hawthorne, sculptor Daniel Chester French, Pulitzer prizewinner Edith Wharton and film stars like Robert De Niro.

9 This huge expanse of water — Lake Champlain, the sixth largest lake in the USA — divides part of Vermont from Canada. Surrounding its shores are gently undulating hills dotted with isolated farmsteads where shiny, ultramodern silos contrast with solid red granaries built in pioneering days.

10 top Some of the most obvious qualities of the Berkshires can be seen in this aerial view: rolling hills, small towns where nature has been left almost undisturbed, scenery that conveys an overwhelming sense of peace and tranquillity. It is hardly surprising that many New Yorkers and Bostonians have vacation homes here.

10 bottom Lake Willoughby, in Vermont, is among the most popular tourist destinations of the Northeast Kingdom. Yachts sail to-and-fro across the lake and, during an Indian summer, the thousands of colours of the surrounding woods are reflected in its clear, unpolluted waters.

12-13 As fall approaches, foliage turns to wondrous shades of yellow, red and gold. It is a beautiful sight, especially in the Berkshires where huddles of white houses, in the typical style of rural Massachusetts, peep out from patches of red and yellow vegetation.

CANADA

St. John River

CANADA

●**Padden**

Chesuncook
Lake

▲*Mt. Katahdin*

Pemadumcook
Lake

West Grand
Lake

Moosehead
Lake

M A I N E

Penobscot

Cobscook Bay

●**Greenville**

Flagstaff
Lake

●**Bangor**

Grand
Manan Island

Kennebec

●**Waterville**

Androsccggin

●**Lewiston** ●**Augusta** Camden
●

Mt. Desert Island
ACADIA NATIONAL PARK

NEW YORK

Champlain
Lake

▲*Mt. Mansfield*

●**Burlington**

Connecticut

Rockland

Isle au Haut

Penobscot Bay

▲*Mt. Washington*

WHITE MOUNTAINS

Sepago
Lake

■**PORTLAND**

V E R M O N T

N E W   H A M P S H I R E

Winnipesaukee
Lake

*Gulf of
Maine*

●**Woodstock**

■**CONCORD** ●**Dover**

MANCHESTER ●**Portsmouth**

Merrimack

ATLANTIC

OCEAN

▲*Mt. Monadnock*

Nashua

●**Pittsfield**

Quabbin
Reservoir

Cambridge
●

Massachusetts Bay

Northampton

■**BOSTON**

M A S S A C H U S E T T S

Cape Cod

■**SPRINGFIELD** ■**WORCESTER**

PROVIDENCE

C O N N E C T I C U T

Rhode
Island

■

**NEW
BEDFORD**

●**Hyannis**

FALL RIVER

Buzzards Bay

HARTFORD

NEWPORT

*Martha's
Vineyard*

Nantucket

■**NEW HAVEN** New London

BRIDGEPORT

Narragansett Bay

●**Greenwich**

Long Island Sound

INTRODUCTION

More than a state, far more than a county, New England came into being thanks to a convention which attributed this name to the historic northeasterly region of the U.S.A. It is in fact comprised of six states — Massachusetts, Connecticut, Rhode Island, Vermont, New Hampshire and Maine — all of them still bearing prominent traces of the early English settlers who first arrived on these shores in 1620 with the Pilgrim Fathers, aboard the "Mayflower". Heading north from New York the first state you encounter is Connecticut, also known as Constitution State since it was the first to sign the constitutional charter on January 14, 1639. The Connecticut landscape is generously dotted with pretty villages and isolated log cabins encompassed

by greenery, making it an ideal place to restore body and spirit from the breakneck pace of big city life: from the lure of old whaling vessels in Mystic Seaport to the more worldly pleasures of downtown Greenwich, its variegated attractions suit diverse lifestyles. Not without good reason has it been called "The Pride of New England". The smallest state in the U.S.A. is Rhode Island, hence its nickname "Little Rhody": it measures only about 50 miles by 40 but its enormous appeal to the pedigreed and seriously wealthy more than compensates for its diminutive size. Newport, for example, with its international sailing regattas, jazz festivals and jet-set tourism, is an elitist summer playground. The tiny shoreline villages are perhaps more rich in atmosphere: a stroll around the streets of Bristol or Portsmouth inevitably becomes a fascinating journey into the past, to the time when Rhode Island was known by its Indian name Aquidneck and Giovanni da Verrazzano, renowned Italian navigator, landed in Narragansett Bay. Maine is the northernmost state, sharing its borders with New Hampshire and Canada: largest of the New England states, the other five could fit within its perimeters. Its big cities may reflect the metropolitan stereotype geared to

14 The Memorial Church in Cambridge commemorates all the Harvard alumni who lost their lives in wars; the church is in Harvard Yard, the oldest part of the university campus.

15 Trinity Church is reflected in the glazed walls of the John Hancock Tower, New England's tallest skyscraper (62 floors). The church was built in the first half of the 1700s and is one of the oldest in the city. It is situated between Boylston and St. James Avenue, in other words, between Chinatown and Back Bay.

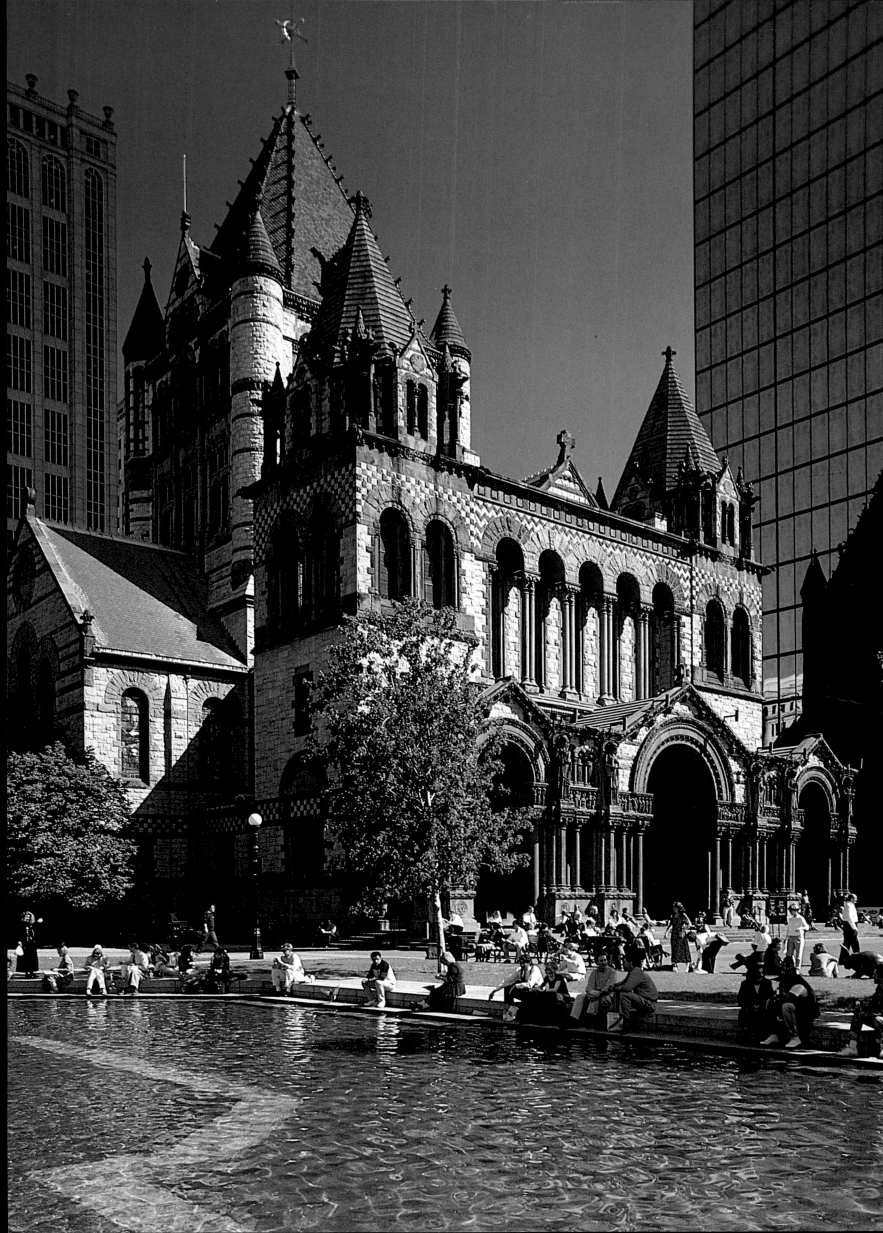

16 top Since as early as 1869 the Cog Railway has been one of the most popular ways of getting up Mount Washington. This little steam train climbs one of the world's steepest slopes at a maximum speed of four miles an hour. Close to the peak is Tip Top House, a stone-built refuge which operated as an inn, and the small Mount Washington museum.

16-17 Thanks to its quiet villages and bracing air, even in the 1800s the White Mountains region became a destination for vacationers. The lodges at the foot of Mount Washington were joined by classy giants like the Mount Washington Hotel at Bretton Woods. With their white walls, red roofs and soaring towers, these buildings look like castles, set in a landscape transformed with each change of season.

skyscrapers and abundant concrete, but here the quintessential architectural model is the weatherboard family homestead. Nature is the protagonist in this region, also known as Pine Tree State. And the natural beauty of its scenery defies description: rugged coasts carved by great glaciers, tongues of land stretching out into the immensity of the Atlantic Ocean, innumerable tiny islands offering visitors full immersion in a natural wonderland, but one with the surveillance and protection implicit in national park status. The mountains of New Hampshire, soaring higher than any others in the north-east, have earned it the name of "Granite State". Much of the charm of its landscape lies in a myriad of lakes large and small (over 1,300 in all) and a coastline slightly less than 20 miles in length but punctuated with historic landmarks. For here in New Hampshire settlers set up their own government and declared independence from Great Britain seven months before the celebrated Fourth of July 1776 when America's Declaration of Independence was signed. This state is also the perfect place for lovers of the great outdoors. Countless activities are possible here: hiking through forests, skiing and snowboarding high in the White Mountains, fishing in the numerous rivers and lakes which still have ancient Native American names — Winnipesaukee, Ossipee, Sunapee — , even close encounters with native fauna, deer and bears for instance… Vermont is the only landlocked state of New England but amply compensating for the lack of ocean are vast woods and forests (covering three-quarters of the state's territory) and consistently beautiful scenery. Scenic splendour reaches its climax in fall when nature is clad in Indian Summer colours and foliage turns every shade of red and yellow. In winter the Green Mountain State, as Vermont is affectionately known, is endowed with plentiful snow, and the skiing resorts that have sprouted here are much frequented. Massachusetts is considered preeminently as the state of Boston but it stretches from New York state to the Atlantic Ocean, embracing a series of amazingly varied land-, town- and

17 top The religious community of the Shakers (the name came from their ritual dances) was founded by Mother Ann, expelled from the Quakers. The Hancock Shaker Village is a testimony to the austere atmosphere that prevailed in this now "extinct" community. It is comprised of about twenty buildings, dated between 1790 and 1916; the Round Stone Barn can be seen in this photo.

18 top The waterfront south of the village of Mystic is surrounded by typical old sheds and wharves: Thomas Oyster House (1874), where oysters were sorted; the lobster shed, where lobster pots were stored; Halfway House, where lifeboat crews met; and the salmon fishing tackle shed (circa 1840).

seascapes: from the tree-clad slopes of the rolling Berkshire Hills to the fertile farmlands of the Connecticut Valley, and on as far as the sandy shores south of Boston. The state that was the birthplace of American Independence is the America of great writers — Nathaniel Hawthorne, Herman Melville, Louisa May Alcott, Jack Kerouac -, of the Pilgrim Fathers, of college campuses that have spawned Nobel prizewinners, of ultra-fashionable beach resorts, Massachusetts has also been home to whalers and witch hunters. The Bay State has provided settings for countless novels and locations for celebrated films; it is the cradle of art in general, and of music in particular: all year round there are full calendars of concerts, plays, etc. in every urban centre, from the smallest towns to the biggest and busiest cities. In no other place in America is there such an abundance of something in short supply throughout the rest of the United States: history. New England witnessed the birth of American independence for it was here that the settlers of the New World had the courage to rebel against British dominion. Gateway to New England, Boston is the only U.S. city that can boast centuries of history and has monumental landmarks to prove it. The balcony of the old State House, seat of His Majesty's governors, has not changed since settlers, tired of paying taxes to the British crown, stood here to read the Declaration of Independence. The date was July 18, 1776. Even the smallest village takes pride in its heritage: Nantucket, for instance, an island of only 50 square miles, has no fewer than 800 buildings protected by the Historic Conservation Board. American history was indeed made in New England, time and time again. The whole nation takes pride in Harvard, the oldest university of the New Continent: situated in Boston, it has produced — and continues to produce — Nobel prizewinners, great ministers and political leaders, top government officials and worldbeating captains of industry; it has been alma mater of many famous names, including Bostonian John Fitzgerald Kennedy. America's second oldest university is also in New England: Yale first

18-19 Mystic Seaport is another open-air museum, offering an authentic picture of life in a 19th century seaboard town where, thanks to an abundant supply of fine-quality timber, shipbuilding was the main activity. More than three hundred 18th and 19th century sailing vessels can be seen in this maritime museum. Moored in the entirely reconstructed harbour is the last whaler made of timber: the Charles W. Morgan, launched in 1841.

19 top Lining the streets of Mystic are old shops: Stone's Store, for instance, selling haberdashery and hardware, the Drugstore (1870), where both pharmacist and doctor were on hand, and Burrow House (1860), a typical seaside cottage with a garden, is also worth a visit.

opened its doors to students in 1701, in New Haven, Connecticut. The "sweet smell" of wealth, power and culture pervades the air of New England and throughout America the names of these universities are synonymous with illustrious professors and education excellence. In the classrooms of Harvard, as in Yale and colleges across the nation, ambition as a fundamental element of competition and success, is instilled in students from the very moment they set foot on the campus: "to be first, you must study, study, and study more". The riches of New England are material as well as cultural: breathtaking villas of millionaires, super-luxury yachts and private islands all speak louder than words. Cape Cod and the islands of Martha's Vineyard and Nantucket are the ultimate retreats and vacation resorts of America's seriously rich and famous: remember the "home movies" of JFK and Jackie relaxing with their children on the beach of the Kennedy clan's stupendous home at Hyannis Port? Further evidence of New England's prosperity is seen in the smart shopping streets of the busiest towns, where glittering windows attract plenty of tourists. None can rival the expensive chic of Boston's Newbury Street: an incredible line-up of prestigious designer boutiques, elegant cafés, craft stores catering strictly for the very well-heeled, antiques dealers offering the finest in American period furniture and silverwares. And New England's seemingly inexhaustible wealth does not end here: nature is surely one of its greatest assets, with huge, thick forests which take on a totally different look in autumn. The patchwork colours of these fertile lands often contribute to the mouthwatering delights of local culinary traditions: the bright red of deliciously flavoured New England cranberries, for instance, grown mainly around Plymouth and Cape Cod, turns fields into stunning ruby-red carpets for tens and tens of miles. The star of the local gastronomic scene is also red: lobsters are a ubiquitous feature of New England cuisine, found everywhere and served at any time of day (even on breakfast menus).

20-21 Dotted along the coast of Maine are numerous lighthouses, solitary sentinels whose light is a precious guide to ships sailing by in the darkness of night. The Portland Head lighthouse is one of the oldest, built in 1791 at the initiative of George Washington, then president of the United States. From the top of the building, 80 feet high, there is a splendid view over Casco Bay and the beams from twelve other lighthouses can be seen on clear nights. The 19th century American poet H.W. Longfellow visited this lighthouse on many occasions and sang its praises in his poems.

22-23 Extending across the western side of Massachusetts, the Berkshire Hills are crossed by a road which links the towns of Stockbridge, Lenox, Pittsfield (in the picture), Williamstown and North Adams. In these out-of-the-way places the natural landscape provides a fitting backdrop for the arts: the Tanglewood concerts in Lenox are just one of many musical, artistic and cultural attractions that draw crowds to the Berkshires.

BOSTON

"In New York they ask how much you earn, in Philadelphia who your parents are, in Boston only what you know": the words of American writer and humorist Mark Twain still ring true today. The people of America acknowledge Boston as the nation's leading city of culture and learning, and also see it ideally as the spiritual capital of the United States. In figures at least, this is borne out by the scientific community installed in the capital of Massachusetts: no fewer than seventy universities and colleges, plus numerous research institutions. Heading this impressive body of learning are, of course, Harvard and the Massachusetts Institute of Technology, better known as MIT. From 1636 to the present day Harvard has been the

alma mater of six U.S. presidents and 30 Nobel prizewinners; MIT is instead unparalleled worldwide as a seedbed of science and technical know-how, ever intent on turning out avant-garde ideas and generations of ruling classes. Many students now seated in these classrooms are destined to eventually become top managers of huge corporations. Each year these giant scientific and cultural institutions bring to Boston over 300,000 students and faculty — one of the largest college and university populations in the world — and their presence conditions city life in many ways. For a start, it makes Boston the youngest city in America: its inhabitants'average age is under 30. The student population is concentrated in Cambridge, an independent city on the far side of the slow-moving Charles River, home of Harvard and college campus par excellence. The atmosphere here is young and vibrant: you have only to look around you when seated in a café or entering one of the 25 bookstores in and around Harvard Square. Traces of "Old America" are liberally scattered all over this dazzling yet pragmatic city. For instance in the lanes of Beacon Hill, the old district built on Boston's highest summit; history and style are also encountered when strolling past the rows

24 Just a matter of yards away from Faneuil Hall Marketplace is the Old State House, Boston's oldest public building (1713), now dwarfed by the high-rise giants on Battery March Street. Every year, on July the Fourth, the Declaration of Independence is read from its balcony.

25 Guests at the Bostonian Hotel have a splendid view over Faneuil Hall Marketplace with its numerous shops and boutiques and tens of restaurants and cafés, all housed in three 19th century structures. This huge pedestrian area is now one of the city's trendiest, with plenty of improvised performances put on by street entertainers.

26 top Many of Boston's buildings were designed by Chinese-American architect I.M. Pei, celebrated worldwide as the creator of the glass pyramid at the Louvre in Paris.

26-27 Viewed from offshore, with its skyscrapers seemingly floating in the Atlantic Ocean, the cityscape of Boston offers a thrilling sight. The vibrant and learned capital of Massachusetts may be the most European place in America and its biggest university city, but it is also — quintessentially — a seaport.

27 top This panoramic view of Boston and the Charles River was taken from Cambridge. A huge campus area — home to the Massachusetts Institute of Technology (MIT) and the prestigious Harvard University — it is connected to Boston by the Harvard Bridge. This extremely long bridge in fact measures 364.4 "smoots", i.e. that many times the height (5'7") of a certain Oliver R. Smoot, a Harvard student in the 1950s, who measured the entire bridge "head-to-heel", to the great amusement of his college buddies.

of Victorian houses along two lovely streets, Mount Vernon and Chestnut. And a tour of classic Boston takes in entire neighbourhoods where narrow roads, on a slight gradient, are paved with red brick and gas lamps stand like sentries outside grand 18th and 19th century homes with distinctive wrought-iron windows: for a moment you might even think yourself in London or Oxford... Imbibing this atmosphere you come to realize another truth about Boston: it is a city where class counts. When writing about Boston and its smartest districts, Henry James described Mount Vernon as the most prestigious address in America: he must have forgotten that in the 18th century the street was nicknamed Mount Whoredom, on account of its many brothels. Today these Victorian mansions are homes of descendants of the "brahmins", aristocratic Boston families who still talk with the pure nasal accent characteristic of early emigrants who left England to settle in the New World. Of some surprise to the residents of Beacon Hill and other upmarket neighbourhoods like Brooklyne is the city's new penchant for glitz and glamour, in no place more evident than on Newbury Street, meeting place of New England's beau monde. Moving in droves around this part of town is Boston's gilded youth, models and Harvard students who gather in the best cafés and shop. Ancient and modern are equally at home in Boston: turning your back on the crowded Newbury Street, you quickly rediscover the atmosphere of the Old Continent, following the Freedom Trail. This 3-mile "fil rouge" — a red line painted on streets and sidewalks — connects sixteen buildings linked with American Independence (the oldest dates back to circa 1660). At every turn, in this part of Boston, you come face to face with major historic sites recalling events which turned this vast country into a great nation: Park Street Church, where the campaign for the abolition of slavery was begun in 1829; State House, the seat of government built in 1795; Old South Meeting House, where the Revolution Museum displays a collection of documents, prints and other Independence memorabilia; Paul Revere House, one-time

home of the patriot who, in April 1775, rode through the night to warn the revolutionaries that English troops had landed. The trail continues to North End, Boston's very oldest district, first occupied by Irish settlers; now living in its 17th and 18th century buildings are Italian immigrants who arrived here in the early years of this century. The influence of the Old Continent is evident in many aspects of the city, for instance in the neo-Gothic ogives of the sombre Trinity Church. Designed by architect Henry Hobson Richardson in 1877, the church reflects its structures on the glazed walls of the John Hancock Tower, with its 62 floors the tallest skyscraper in New England. From the vantage point afforded by this giant there is a splendid 360° view over the city, its old houses and the winding course of the Charles River which divides Boston in two. Not only does the city have a plethora of sites commemorating America's glorious past; you can even go back in time and re-live salient moments of history. Moored in calm water by Congress Street Bridge is a replica of one of the famous "Boston Tea Party" ships: come aboard and recall the time when Bostonians rebelled against the British by dumping shiploads of tea in the harbour. Politics and power also count for a lot in Boston, a fact echoed in a comment on Bostonians' political convictions made by Eugene O'Neill, celebrated playwright and native of the city, who said that here newborn babes are first registered to vote, and then baptized. Many Bostonians have risen to the top of the American power structure and left their mark on the nation's history but none has achieved greater fame and celebrity status than John Fitzgerald Kennedy. The JFK Library Museum was erected by the people of Boston as a token of their affection for a much-admired President. Collected together in this all-white building, with window-walls overlooking the ocean, are documents testifying to the most important events in the life of the 35th President of the United States of America, from his election until his death in Dallas at the hands of a gunman, in 1963. But Boston also has a rich and varied cultural life — it has even been called

28 top The resemblance between this building and the White House in Washington is quick to spot. In actual fact the same architect, Charles Bulfinch, also designed the gilt dome of the new State House in Boston, built in 1798.

28 bottom On the corner of Park and Tremont Streets, Park Street Church stands encircled by skyscrapers, its spire pointing upwards like a spear: a defiant challenge to its high-rise neighbours. The church has in fact never been short of courage. During the War of 1812 it was known as Brimstone Corner, since its vault was used to store gunpowder.

29 Boston is a city where old and new live in harmony. In the foreground is the Old State House, built as seat of the Colonial government in 1713 and still decorated with the insignia of the British crown. It was in front of this building that British troops opened fire on the rebellious people of Boston in 1770, and from its balcony the "Declaration of Independence" was read.

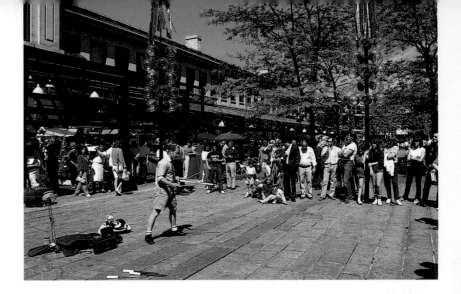

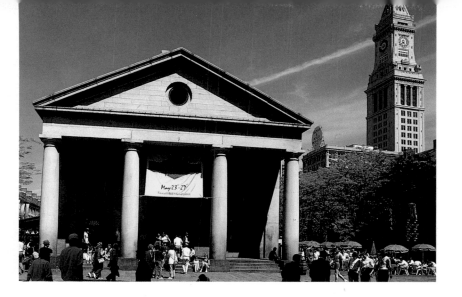

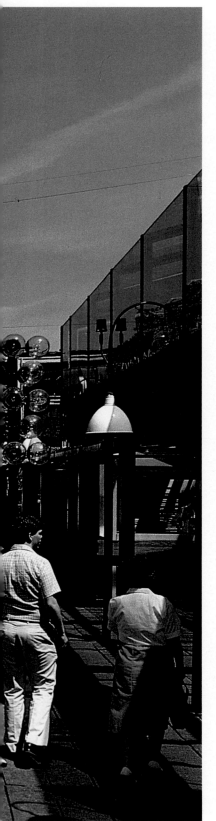

the "Athens of America". With plentiful art exhibitions, theatrical productions, concerts, etc., the creative minds of the capital of Massachusetts have much to inspire them. An impressive collection of artworks is housed in the Isabella Stewart Gardner Museum. Born in New York and a Bostonian by marriage, Isabella Stewart Gardner adored Italian art; in 1899 this millionaire spared no expense when building Fenway Court, in 15th century Venetian style, and filling it with art treasures. Its eclectic contents are now on show to the public and range from textiles, ceramics and furniture to paintings by Raphael, Titian, Mantegna, Masaccio, Pier della Francesca. At the Computer Museum many exhibits are of the hands-on variety: kids (and grown-ups too) can enrich their minds while playing on countless computers at their disposal: you can interact with a PC, change your personal appearance on a video display, drive a Formula One racing car or sink into the world of virtual reality. In Boston learning is really made fun: at home in the gigantic observation tank of the New England Aquarium are numerous species of sea creatures, including turtles, seals, penguins, sea lions and sharks. Should you want to admire the giants of the ocean in their natural habitat, you can take a trip on a whale-watching cruise: about half-hour after leaving harbour, the huge forms of these leviathans of the deep already come into view. Boston Bay is well-known for its whale "traffic", and it apparently offers an ideal environment for breeding. Another typically Bostonian passion is music: the city Symphony Orchestra was founded in 1881 under the auspices of philanthropist Henry Lee Higginson and its concerts are events not to be missed. Jazz has a big following in the city too: jam sessions organized by students of the Berklee College of Music attract crowds of regulars and in the Berklee Performance Center the auditorium resounds with warbling voices or the notes of a saxophone. In other words, Boston always has something new to offer. And should the city ever convey a feeling of déjà vu, don't let it worry you: that familiar-looking scene is obviously something you already saw at the movies.

30-31 In Quincy Market there are jugglers and conjurors on practically every corner. Approached through a refurbished neo-classical structure, this pedestrian precinct is an ideal place for strolling as well as shopping: its one hundred and more outlets are mainly small shops, selling everything from hand-crafted articles to tastebud-tempting Bostonian specialities. Quincy Market is the main building of a larger shopping complex. Faneuil Hall Marketplace, filled with a vast assortment of cafés, restaurants and boutiques which keep the area thronging with people at practically every hour of the day and night. With its busy, vibrant atmosphere it is perhaps one of the most popular and trendy places in town; it is certainly an outstanding example of how a sensible urban renewal policy can breathe new life into previously run-down parts of town.

32 top This part of the city was once beneath the waters of the Charles River. In 1856 work began on a reclamation and construction scheme that took thirty years to complete. The area formerly occupied by the tidal mud flats of Back Bay is now — culturally and socially — one of the liviest parts of Boston.

Its main thoroughfare is the elegant and upmarket Newbury Street, with its succession of trendy eating places, smart cafés and designer boutiques. This is the place where fashions are set, frequented by "anybody who's anybody", often making sure their presence is noticed.

32-33 Boston may be the cradle of the United States as a nation but it is the least American city of the New World. Its style is thoroughly European, and aristocratic too: an impression immediately confirmed when admiring the delightful houses of Beacon Hill, Boston's smartest district. Each house and street recalls something of the atmosphere of Old England.

33 top The New Old South Church overlooks Copley Square. Nearby is Copley Place, ideal for indoor shopping: its galleries offer a wide assortment of stores, selling just about everything.

33 bottom Acorn Street is the most photographed street in the city. The houses lining this narrow street, almost an alley, were built in 1828/29. In 1991 Acorn Street's cobbles were taken up to allow construction work, stored away and, once the work was completed, carefully re-laid one by one. In recent years residents in this charming street have included the Kennedys, Henry Kissinger and the Aga Khan.

34-35 Most banks and insurance companies have their headquarters in downtown Boston. Towering over every other skyscraper is the Prudential Center.

36 At sunset, clouds are mirrored in the blue glazed walls of the John Hancock Tower (named after a patriotic and wealthy citizen of 18th century Boston). The Skywalk observatory offers breathtaking views of the city.

37 The Charles River separates Cambridge from Boston. The riverside is a favourite place to go jogging, and canoeing is currently all the rage. October is the month of the "Head of the Charles Regatta" and, for Bostonians, the 22nd is a particularly important date, when some of the world's major canoeing events are held here: as well as college teams, there are canoeists from clubs in every corner of the globe. Races start at 8 p.m. and continue until about 4 p.m. Would-be spectators determined to get a good view of the events from the riverbank are advised to get there very early.

38 top and 38-39 Pictured here is the headquarters complex of the Christian Science Church and Mother Church. Intellectual snobbery is one of Boston's better known traits. Feud of the Kennedys and home to exponents of the upscale U.S. cultural scene, the city is now a favourite destination among American travellers: its airport facilities and incoming flights are expected to double by the end of the century.

38 centre The USS Constitution is moored near Charlestown Bridge. During the War of 1812 this sailing ship was engaged in no fewer than 44 battles against the British and survived undamaged, earning the nickname of Old Ironsides. Now a floating museum, she is well worth a visit and can still sail out to sea, though for only a few miles.

38 bottom Boston Common is the city's largest public park. Its pond has swan boats on which to take leisurely cruises, and turns into a skating rink when iced over in winter. The Freedom Trail, marked by a red stripe along the sidewalk, starts from Boston Common, where there is a Visitor Information Center.

39 top Hanover Street is the main thoroughfare of Boston's "Little Italy": in the North End district of the city, the area's many Italian restaurants, groceries, pizza joints and cafés with unbeatable cappuccino attract Bostonians and tourists alike. In the Café Sport, for example, you can order delicious Sicilian pastries and Sambuca "con la mosca" (served with a coffee bean or two floating on the surface).

40 bottom The interior of the Isabella Stewart Gardner Museum is smart and unusual. Actually a New Yorker, Isabella Stewart married the rich Bostonian John Lowel Gardner. In her artistic taste she was influenced by the art critic Bernard Berenson. In her will Isabella Stewart specified that the house remain packed with its art treasures, arranged as she had left them.

40 top First established in Copley Square in 1876, the Museum of Fine Arts boasts priceless artworks from every period of history. Its exhibits are divided into six sections: Asian art, Egyptian art, Classical art, American art, European decorative arts and European paintings. Its collections grew so large that, at the beginning of the 1900s, a new museum was built to house them, in Huntington Avenue.

40-41 Through a glass roof light streams into the enclosed courtyard of the Isabella Stewart Gardner Museum. The courtyard is her own original creation: the flowers planted here are changed at every season, to ensure the garden is ablaze with colour all year round. There are Bostonians who can afford to buy a Venetian palazzo, have it dismantled, shipped back home and then rebuilt here: such was the case of the super-rich Isabella Stewart Gardner. She bequeathed the building and its contents to the city of Boston, and it was subsequently turned into a museum.

41 top The Museum of Fine Arts has an important collection of Egyptian artworks: much of this evidence of over 4,000 years of civilization came to light during excavations conducted over a period of 40 years, initiated in 1905 in collaboration with Harvard University.

41 bottom Visitors to the Isabella Stewart Gardner Museum are not only impressed by the fine collection of paintings (including works by Botticelli, Raphael and Titian), sculptures, carpets and pottery; they also savour the unique ambience created by a Venetian palace transplanted in a 20th century metropolis.

42-43 Not far from Harvard Square is the university's Memorial Hall, which looks surprisingly like a church. Part of the building was used as a refectory, part was divided into class-rooms. An amusing anecdote about Harvard: the millionairess who donated the funds to build the university library, the world's largest, laid down two conditions: not a single brick was to be moved, and all students enrolled at Harvard had to know how to swim.

42 top and bottom, 43 top Harvard is America's oldest university, founded in 1636. Among its alumni are six presidents of the USA, 33 Nobel prizewinners and 31 Pulitzer prizewinners. Welcoming visitors to this giant educational institution is the statue of lies. Engraved in its marble is a brief epithet containing three falsehoods: "John Harvard, founder, 1638". John Harvard was not the university's founder but its benefactor, the year of its foundation was not 1638 but 1636, and the statue actually depicts an anonymous student. A popular way to do some reading is stretched out on the lawn of Harvard Yard (the only American campus to use the English term) or seated on the imposing steps leading up to the library.

44-45 The Massachusetts Institute of Technology — known worldwide as MIT — is about 3 miles south of Harvard Square and the contrast with the architecture and atmosphere of Harvard is striking. Its campus was clearly designed by and for scientists, as it is evident in the Atmospheric and Planetary Sciences Building (right top). In these austere buildings with their Doric colonnades, the first computer was designed, in 1929; in this oasis of peace, the Patriot missile was perfected and research that eventually led to the conquest of space was started. Scattered around the campus are important collections of contemporary sculpture, with works by preeminent artists: Picasso, Moore, Calder. Several buildings are of outstanding architectural interest, like the Kresge Auditorium by Eero Saarinen (right bottom).

46-47 The historic part of Boston has the same shape than your left hand. From the wrist forward it is surrounded on three sides by water: north-west, the Charles River divides it from the campus city of Cambridge, where Harvard University and the MIT are situated; north and north-east, the port bay, opening out onto the Atlantic Ocean, separates it from Charlestown and Logan Airport; south-east, Fort Point Channel marks the border with the black district of South Boston. At the very top of the clenched wrist, all around the finger joints, are the docks, North End, an old district and an Italian enclave, the Government Center district and Quincy Market. Practically in the very centre of the back of your hand is Boston Common, which originated as long ago as the 1700s.

THE COAST

The New England seaboard has a lyrical beauty: thundering waves breaking on rocky shores, rolling sand dunes adorned with bushes red with cranberries, many-towered mansions reminiscent of French châteaux, white clapboard cottages and waterfront chalets with landing-stages, codfishing trawlers outlined on the distant horizon. The seascapes of the coastal region appear to be poised on the brink of stillness and melancholy: the sea can be rough, swept by storms, or lost in swirling, ever-thicker mists; profiled against the horizon are tall lighthouses, strategically positioned along the shore. Down the coast of Maine these sentinels of the ocean signal a possible route, projecting meaningful beams of light that pierce the

darkness and are — still today — a precious navigational aid to shipping. Thomas Duffon, an officer with the U.S. Coast Guard, likens the lighthouses of Maine to the castles of Europe and indeed, the majority of them have conserved their original structures. The most powerful is at Cape Elizabeth, the most easterly at Quoddy Head, the most isolated on a tiny island just off the coast of Camdem, between Rockport and Rockland. Not far from New York state are the great cities of the Connecticut coastline, fronting the Atlantic Ocean: for instance, Bridgeport, an essentially industrial city celebrated mainly for an illustrious past resident, circus impresario Phineas T. Barnum, or history-rich New Haven. But it is in the village of Mystic, on the Mystic River, not far from New London, that the influence of maritime history on American life, and on this part of America in particular, is revealed in all its glory. This outdoor museum offers a meticulously detailed insight into lifestyles in a seaboard town, with exhibits ranging from nautical repair workshops and lobster fishing tackle to assorted sea-going vessels, including a fully equipped whaler. Leaving behind the historic sailing ships of the pioneering world of New England's first settlers, you can travel through time into a futuristic age: the wonders of

48-49 Fine sand and clear waters characterize the east coast of the peninsula of Cape Cod (Massachusetts), stretching 120 miles from Chatman to Provincetown. A splendid oasis of unspoiled nature, the Cape Cod National Seashore, protected since 1961, covers 28,000 acres of land, crowned by an endless array of spectacular sand-dunes. The peninsula also witnessed its share of history: it was here, in 1602, that one of the region's first explorers, Bartholomew Gosnold, first set foot on American soil, and was immediately struck by the huge quantities of cod he saw swimming in these waters. And it was also here — in fact on the site where Provincetown was later founded — that the Mayflower landed in 1620, with its shipload of Pilgrims who proceeded to colonize the region. In the 19th century Cape Cod became an important centre of the whaling industry, although its perilous waters claimed tens of ships every year (even today, at low tide, wrecks of numerous vessels which went down before Cape Cod Canal was built can be seen emerging from the ocean).

advanced technology are revealed at the U.S. Coast Guards Academy of New London where visitors can tour the "Eagle", a sailing ship used by the cadets, and even a nuclear submarine. Further along the coast, in Massachusetts, is New Bedford which, until the mid-1800s, disputed the title of whaling capital with the nearby island of Nantucket. From its origins as a small fishing village New Bedford developed into a centre of international trade; it remained important for over a hundred years, until the discovery of oil in Pennsylvania and the loss of many ships from its fleet consigned it to oblivion once more. Among the finest gems dotted along this stretch of coastline is undoubtedly Cape Cod — a tongue of land about 40 miles long — situated in a truly enviable position, between Boston and New York. The place has long been the vacation refuge of millionaires: hidden amid the woods around Hyannis, carefully disguised by hedges and flower-decked gardens, are the homes of America's most wealthy men. It is no coincidence that the Kennedy family chose Hyannis Port as the resort in which to spend the most carefree and serene periods of their life. John Fitzgerald Kennedy too John Fitzgerald Kennedy too considered Cape Code his own special retreat; of this haven of peace and quiet he said: "I always come back to the Cape and walk the beach when I have a tough decision to make. The Cape is one place where I can think and be alone". A more bohemian population of artists and intellectuals has also settled in Cape Cod, mainly in Provincetown, on the very tip. About 30 miles further south are the two islands which, with Cape Cod, form an ideal triangle of elite vacation sites: Martha's Vineyard and Nantucket. Martha's Vineyard is fairly large, with an area of 95 square miles; Nantucket, where a more reserved atmosphere prevails, is about half the size. But both are renowned for clear blue water, fine sands on which to soak up the sun's rays, waves that beg you to get onto your surfboard, picturesque fisherman's cottages and quaint little restaurants, all timbers and brass, where they serve delicious shrimps and, of course, wonderful lobsters. Many

50-51 In colonial times the seaboard village of York — originally called Aqamenticus — was a place of refuge for Anglicans and royalists; nowadays its long sandy beaches attract vacationers from Philadelphia or nearby Boston.

50 top and 51 top Mist and fog spell danger for sailors travelling along the jagged coastline of Maine, scattered with peninsulas, headlands, inlets and rocks lurking just below the surface. On days when visibility is close to nil, it is only thanks to the sirens and flashing lights of lighthouses that ships find their way into harbour. Pictured here is the lighthouse on Bailey Island.

52 top and 53 top Located at the very tip of Cape Ann, Rockport is an old fishing village which derives its name from the long-gone local granite quarries. During the war of secession it became a colony of well-known artists who brought a certain air of originality to the place. There is still a notable concentration of art galleries — interspersed with craft stores and little shops — in the Bearskin Neck area, close to Dock Square.

tucked-away corners of Martha's Vineyard are often off-limits. Their beaches are strictly private, havens for the celebrities — mostly movie stars — who come here to stay in Victorian-style mansions where they can "get away from it all", particularly from prying eyes. Their homes generally stand in vast grounds, with plenty of room for the helicopters that allow VIPs like Woody Allen, Dustin Hoffman, Steven Spielberg to come and go without even being noticed. Thanks to its popularity with the reigning Hollywood set, Martha's Vineyard has acquired the image of the most glamorous island of the entire U.S. Atlantic coast. The island's unusual name is said to be linked with Bartholomew Gosnold, the British navigator who made the first recorded landing here, back in 1602; he noticed the wild vines that then grew here in abundance and chose this name for the island, after his daughter Martha. Of those once-thriving vines there is now no longer trace. Light years away from the beau monde of Martha's Vineyard is the island of Nantucket which, in the Amerindian language, means "distant land": the atmosphere that pervades the town streets, lined with old — and amazing well preserved — grey houses, still smacks of the early colonial era. Here, in the 17th century, American Indians taught the new settlers how to harpoon whales which passed just a short way from the shore. And it was here that Herman Melville set some of the most thrilling passages of his famous novel, "Moby Dick". Strolling along the waterfront it is not hard to conjure up mental pictures of those bygone days when cargo ships set sail from Nantucket for the Old Continent. Stacked in their holds were barrels of precious whale-oil, used to light the streets of glittering cities like London, Paris... Today Nantucket is also famous for its beaches, over 90 miles of fine sand lapped by water made warmer by the Gulf Stream. Gazing across this placid stretch of ocean it seems hardly possible that Nantucket was once one of the world's foremost whaling ports and that at times the breakers were ruby-red with the blood of these innocent creatures. The chilly waters of the Atlantic which hug the

52-53 The northernmost seaboard town in Massachusetts is Newburyport, where characteristic redbrick houses were once the homes of merchants and sea captains. And the town and its small harbour still conserve a 19th century atmosphere. Ten miles south of Newburyport is Plum Island, a narrow spit of land which, as well as a wildlife refuge, has some of the loveliest and wildest beaches in New England.

New England

55 The coast of Maine extends for no fewer than 3,500 miles (but 250 miles as the crow flies), with variegated scenery: straight sandy beaches in the south, deep inlets and coves around Boothbay Harbor and sprinklings of islands like Monhegan and Mount Desert Island. From Kittery, Coastal Route 1 follows the ins and outs of the coastline, as far as the Canadian border.

54 top Cadillac Mountain is on the eastern side of Mount Desert Island, not far from the spectacular cliffs of Otter Point. Discovered by Samuel de Champlain in 1605, the island is part of Acadia National Park and it is reckoned to be one of the least spoiled natural landscapes in America.

54 bottom Towards the end of June Boothbay Harbor in Maine bustles with celebrations for the annual Windjammer Days. This picturesque little town welcomes practically a fleet of schooners, the graceful sailing vessels that once plied the waters of the Atlantic Ocean with their cargoes of timber. These ships are also stars of the Great Schooner Race, the famous regatta held in nearby Rockland.

seaboard of Massachusetts also wash the shores of Salem, the city which earned a place in history-books thanks to the only witchcraft trials ever held on American soil. In 1692, stimulated by voodoo tales told by a West Indian slave Tituba, many young girls of Salem claimed to have had strange visions. A doctor who examined them said they were possessed by the devil and, at a time when religious fanaticism fanned such beliefs, the atmosphere in the town was close to hysteria. Over 150 suspects were quickly accused and tried for witchcraft: 19 convicted "witches" were even hanged. New Hampshire has only one port: Portsmouth. A colonial capital until 1808, this quiet town was founded in 1623 by English settlers, attracted by the wild strawberries which grew in abundance along the shores close to the mouth of the Piscataqua river: its original name was Strawbery Banke. The "Port at the Mouth of the River" is still a peaceful place, proud of the now carefully preserved heritage of its past. In Maine, today as centuries ago, the ocean means fishing: from March to the end of December myriads of fishing boats put out to sea, from ports as large as Portland or as small as Boothbay Harbor; they haul up their wooden lobster pots and return with them neatly arrayed in tanks brimful with water. A superb way to survey the rare beauty of this untamed corner of the globe is to cruise along the coast on board a schooner, one of the old windjammers built in the late 19th century to ship lumber to seaboard towns. Through the centuries Portland, Maine's largest city, has experienced more than its fair share of troubles, rising — no fewer than three times — like a phoenix from the ashes. It has nonetheless retained its typically waterfront character and charm and, while trade has a major role in its economy, history and tradition are keynotes of its underlying cultural fabric. For sea-lovers this stretch of the Atlantic offers another thrilling experience: whale-watching from one of the cruise vessels that leave Bar Harbor on Mount Desert Island; after as little as two hours heading out towards the open sea, the huge humped backs of polar whales can already be spotted on the horizon.

56-57 Lobster fishing is a mainstay of Maine's economy. Huge quantities of these delicious crustaceans are found on the rocky floors of the ocean, where the water is cold and clear. Fishermen leave their lobster-pots in place, marking their position with coloured buoys. Each fisherman has his own colour, to ensure that the pots — and their contents — are retrieved by their rightful owner.

56 top and bottom From the chilly floor of the Atlantic to a pan of boiling water: to be tasted at its best lobster must still be alive when dropped into the boiling water, and a tiny shack along the sea shore is the ideal place to eat it. This does not mean you cannot enjoy the authentic flavour elsewhere: "packed-to-travel" lobster stays fresh for hours.

57 top Lobster — hallowed by epicurians the world over — is the gastronomic symbol of New England. Many towns and villages along the coast of Maine organize an annual Lobster Festival, a worthy pretext for song & dance, sports events and parades all held in honour of the venerated crustacean which is served, boiled or steamed, with sweetcorn and melted butter.

58 A late-evening mist descends over fishing boats and yachts moored in one of the many bays of Acadia National Park. The park covers an area of 110 square miles and includes Mount Desert Island, Isle au Haut and other neighbouring islets.

59 Mount Desert Island harbours most of Acadia National Park. Here silence and nature reign supreme. Situated on one of the globe's main migratory routes, the island is a paradise for birdwatchers and other nature lovers.

60-61 From the harbours of Mount Desert Island (Bar Harbor, Northeast Harbor and Bass Harbor), in Acadia National Park, it is possible to take a boat to islands further off the beaten track, to look for eagles'nests and traces of seals.

60 A winding road loops its way around Mount Desert Island, in Acadia National Park, passing close to spectacular sites like Thunder Hole, where the Atlantic waves break noisily on the walls of the cave. The summit of Mount Cadillac affords a breathtaking view over the myriad of islands in Frenchman Bay below.

61 top Depicted here is
another phase in fishing
lobsters: weighing. Once
captured and hauled to the
surface, the lobsters are kept
in cages and immersed in
tanks of water, ready to be
sold on reaching the harbour.

62 top and 63 Among the narrow streets and characteristic houses by the waterfront of New Bedford it is not unusual to encounter old fishermen: their accent is Portuguese, inherited from the army of ship-boys and fishermen who immigrated from Europe to work on whalers. The New Bedford Whaling Museum testifies to the glorious past of the city, for many decades world capital of the whaling industry. Occupying a key place in the museum is Ernestina, the 1824 schooner which was the first to reach the Arctic.

62 centre The exhibits in the Whaling Museum — paintings, tools, equipment, weapons, scrimshaw — take visitors back to the golden age of whaling, as it was described by Herman Melville in his famous novel, "Moby Dick". Shown here is "Whaling a Sperm Whale", painted in 1815; it is one of many artworks on display in the museum.

62 bottom Objects, instruments and arms conserved in the Whaling Museum — and particularly carved or engraved articles made from wood or whalebone (scrimshaw) — give an idea of how sailors spent their days on board one of the many whalers which plied the waters of the Atlantic, constantly on the lookout for whales to hunt.

64-65 The island of Nantucket — an Indian word meaning "distant land" — still retains the atmosphere and charm of bygone days, when its fleet of whaleboats was the finest in the world. It was from the port of Nantucket that Captain Christopher Hussey had set sail when he hunted down a whale in 1712, the first recorded capture by an American boat.

64 top First settled in 1659, Nantucket was essentially a farming community until it turned its attention to seafaring activities. The town has changed little through the centuries. The historic district, downtown, is the most picturesque part: cobbled streets, cottages clad with slate tiles in traditional white, grey or red, and little shops with hand-painted signs.

64 bottom Sankaty Head lighthouse, perched above the village of Siasconset (called 'Sconset), was a point of reference for whaleboats setting out on whaling expeditions. Once a Quaker fishing village of green cedarwood cottages, Siasconset now counts many celebrities in search of privacy among its population.

65 top left Robert Ratliff — a sailor born in Newcastle-upon-Tyne, in England, in 1794 — was a member of the crew which, in 1815, escorted Napoleon to exile on St. Helena. He was also on board the Albion which attacked the city of Washington. Shipwrecked off Nantucket in 1820, he remained there until his death in 1883.

65 top right The legends and adventures of heroic whale hunters are brought to life by authentic relics and assorted memorabilia exhibited at the Whaling Museum in Nantucket, housed in a 19th century candle factory. Visible in the foreground is the jaw bone of a whale.

NEW ENGLAND

66-67 and 66 top Close to the old harbour — in past centuries constantly bustling with the activities of sailors and whalers — is a marina where wealthy residents moor their luxury boats. Nantucket has much to appeal to tourists, not least a stunning landscape, quiet beaches and water warmed by the Gulf Stream.

66 bottom A splendid, solitary spit of sand, Great Point is the northernmost tip of the island. These unspoiled places are the habitat of many species of wildlife.

67 top There are perilous shoals in the waters around Nantucket: in 1956 the liner Andrea Doria sank just fifty miles from its shores and, shortly after World War II, the famous American battleship Missouri ran aground here.

68 top Strawbery Banke —
the historic district of
Portsmouth where the first
settlers put down roots in
1630 — is now an outdoor
museum, in Marcy Street,
where the heritage of this
seafaring city is brought
to life.

68-69 Founded in 1695, the
city of Portsmouth was once
capital of New Hampshire
and its shipyards built
vessels for the Royal Navy. It
reached the peak of fame and
prosperity only in the 1800s
when it became a leading
centre for the construction of
sailing boats. Shown in this
picture are the port and
Memorial Bridge.

69 top Situated on a peninsula close to the mouth of the Piscataqua River, Portsmouth still boasts numerous fine Colonial buildings, many dating back to the early 1800s. In the Old Harbor district, formed of Bow Street (pictured here), Market Street and Ceres Street, are many restaurants, crafts shops and antiques outlets, all recently restored: a reminder of the long-important role of commerce in New Hampshire's port.

69 centre This Georgian residence in Pleasant Street, built in 1784, owes its fame to its first owner: John Langdon was the first president of the U.S. Senate, as well as first governor of New Hampshire.

69 bottom Over thirty period buildings in the oldest part of Portsmouth (Goodwin Mansion, in the photo, is one of them) are still well preserved and entrusted to the care of local residents.

70 top Whale-watching is the favourite sport on the stretch of ocean facing Provincetown, on the extreme tip of Cape Cod. Between April and October these huge mammals come close to shore, looking for plancton; fin whales, humpbacks and white dolphins can be seen swimming just a short distance from passing boats and, in the mating season, their stunning leaps and dives provide extra thrills for onlookers.

70 centre The seascapes of Provincetown are typical of Cape Cod. Formed when glaciers melted, and shaped by wind and waves, the peninsula abounds in woods, ponds, grassy marshes, sand dunes and hills on which peaceful villages perch.

70 bottom Commercial Street is a busy thoroughfare stretching the whole length of Provincetown, the most crowded and vibrant place on Cape Cod, where shops and eating places abound. In the summer months a motley assortment of tourists — prevalently artists, bohemians and rich vacationers — descends on the town, swelling the population to 75,000; off-season a quieter life can be enjoyed by its 3,500 permanent residents.

71 Cape Cod, first landing place of the Pilgrim Fathers when they reached America, is a peninsula with an area of 390 square miles which extends at right-angles into the Atlantic. It derived its name from the abundant cod still fished in its waters.

72-73 Provincetown harbour is a favourite stopping-place for upscale vessels of every shape and size, especially during the summer months when fishermen are obliged to share jetties and mooring cables with yachtsmen.

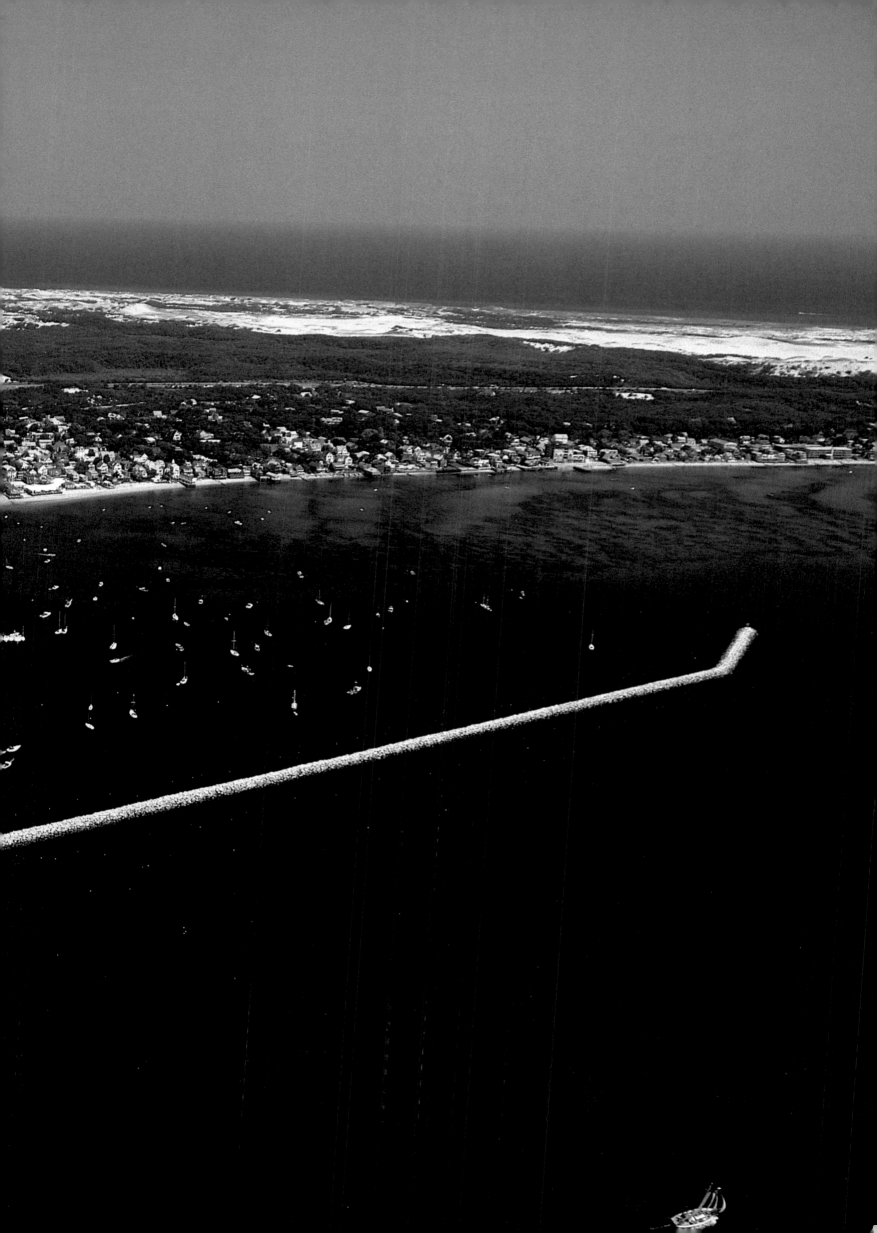

NEWPORT

Mere mention of the name of Newport triggers mental images of boats and regattas, crowned by the glorious America's Cup. But this attractive town is more than a symbol of sailing and unadulterated affluence; it also played a major role in the early history and economic growth of the United States. The first settlers to make their home on this site were a motley band led by William Coddington; he left Boston and sailed south into Narragansett Bay, landing on the southern tip of Aquidneck Island. Newport experienced its economic heydey before the Revolution, when its port was a hive of activity as ships unloaded and loaded goods in preparation for journeys that took them across the globe. Its greatest source of

prosperity was so-called triangular trade: boats carrying cargoes of rum set sail from Newport for Africa where the liquor was exchanged for slaves; these were then taken to the West Indies and paid for inkind with molasses, fundamental ingredient in the production of rum. Now focal point of Newport sailing events, the harbour is a delightful and well-sheltered spot, blessed by the nearby Atlantic with ideal winds for sailing enthusiasts, who nowadays brave the ocean solely for the joy of it. Is it mere coincidence that the first man to sail around the world singlehanded chose to finish his journey in Newport? Maybe not. The now legendary Joshua Slocum set sail on April 25, 1895, aged 51, on board the 30-foot sloop "Spray", built from the remains of an abandoned wreck. After three years' navigation he arrived in Newport: he had covered a distance of 46,000 miles in complete solitude, with no radio, engine or instrumentation. Slocum was driven by his love of the sea: "The Spray did not sail in search of new worlds, or to relate idle yarns about the perils of the ocean. Wherever my boat took me, I was content". Today Newport is considered capital of the elitist social whirl but even before the Revolution it was regarded as the ideal destination for vacationers: wealthy

74 Rosecliff, one of the most stunning mansions on Bellevue Avenue, was built for Mrs. Hermann Oelrichs in 1902. Designed by famous architect Stanford White, it was modelled after Marie-Antoinette's Petit Trianon in Versailles. Rosecliff's claim to fame was further heightened after Hollywood chose it as the setting for "The Great Gatsby", starring Robert Redford.

75 Founded in 1639 by settlers fleeing from Puritanism in search of greater religious freedom, Newport became one of the great seaports of the colonies. After occupation by the English in 1776 this flourishing hub of trade suffered a serious decline. Not until the early 1800s did its economy pick up: this time the city was turned into a millionaires' playground frequented by aristocrats and super-rich industrialists who, during Newport's so-called Gilded Age, built their fabulous summer mansions along its shores.

76-77 During the colonial era, the port and its settlement became symbols of freethinking and tolerance. Followers of many religious movements flocked to this "new port", drawn by the example of Roger Williams who, exiled from Boston, founded Providence as a refuge from Puritan intolerance.

landowners from Georgia and Carolina came here to escape from the torrid heat of Southern summers. During its Gilded Age Newport became a popular site for fabulous mansions, built for families with highsounding names like Astor, Belmont and Vanderbilt, titans who amassed huge fortunes and were instrumental in America's growth as the world's foremost trading power. "Life is too easy here", they say in Rhode Island's capital of high society and chic. A stroll through downtown Newport puts you in touch with the town's more interesting and less obvious attractions: Thames Street, for instance, is flanked by low buildings of the Colonial era, their façades painted in pastel shades, old England style. Alongside fine examples of America's heritage are the windows of boutiques displaying the very latest New York fashions. In various parts of town are examples of styles typical of American buildings from the mid-17th to late 19th century: the linear forms of the Friends Meeting House where Quakers used to gather, as early as 1699, or Trinity Church, an architectural gem dating back to 1726. But in terms of elegance of design and ornate detail, the grand homes built for the rich and famous offer amazing evidence of one-upmanship. Cliff Walk, a 3-mile trail along a narrow cliff path, takes you back into the realm of unspoiled nature, though you will see many incredibly splendid mansions en route , for example The Breakers, built in Renaissance style in 1885 for Cornelius Vanderbilt II, grandson of "Commodore" Vanderbilt who made his immense fortune from railroads and steamships. Other stunning residences include Marble House, The Elms built by coal "king" Edward Julius Berwind, Rosecliff, Château-sur-Mer in Second Empire style, Belcourt Castle, Hammersmith Farm — home of the Kennedys — , the neo-Gothic Kingscote, and Beechwood, a small stretch of Mediterranean coast transplanted here for the pleasure of William and Caroline Astor. Gusts of wind sweeping off the Atlantic fill your lungs with briny sea air along the 6 miles of Ocean Drive, a succession of viewpoints over extraordinary seascapes, such as Aquidneck Point.

76 top and 77 It was thanks to sailing that Newport became known to sports lovers (and VIP-watchers). Its combination of well-protected harbour and constant winds blowing off the nearby ocean made it one of the world's major centres for this sport: the America's Cup and Sail Newport Regatta are just two of the major sailing events held here. It also has numerous yacht clubs: for instance, the Ida Lewis Yacht Club (top left) in Brenton Cove, one of the city's most exclusive, and the Newport Yacht Club, based at the harbour.

78 top In the gardens of Marble House is a Chinese teahouse where the mistress of the mansion once served her guests afternoon tea (brought to the pagoda from the kitchens on a tiny railway line).

78 centre One of the marvels of Marble House is the Gold Room, its walls entirely covered with gilt stuccowork, marble and mirrors. During the Gilded Age, the most prestigious names of America's aristocracy — the Vanderbilts, Astors, Belmonts, plus a select few members of the socialite scene — gathered in this ballroom to dance the nights away.

78 bottom The Dining Room of the Marble House exudes opulence and wealth: their glitzy surroundings must have left dinner guests wide-eyed — and open-mouthed...

79 Marble House was designed by Richard M. Hunt for the millionaire William Vanderbilt. Completed in 1892, it is one of the most spectacular mansions on Bellevue Avenue. Entirely furnished with original antiques, it gets its name from the huge amount of finest-quality marble used in its construction and decoration.

80-81 Bowen's Wharf could be defined as the hub of the old port of Colonial Newport; its waterfront warehouses, their walls until recently eroded by salt water, have now been renovated and converted into chic eating-places and boutiques.

82-83 Into the huge dock area of Newport — during the colonial period — sailed ships carrying cargoes of molasses, used to produce rum in the city's distilleries (at one time there were no fewer than twenty-two of them). Stowed aboard ships bound for Africa, the rum was later used by slave traders as payment for slaves.

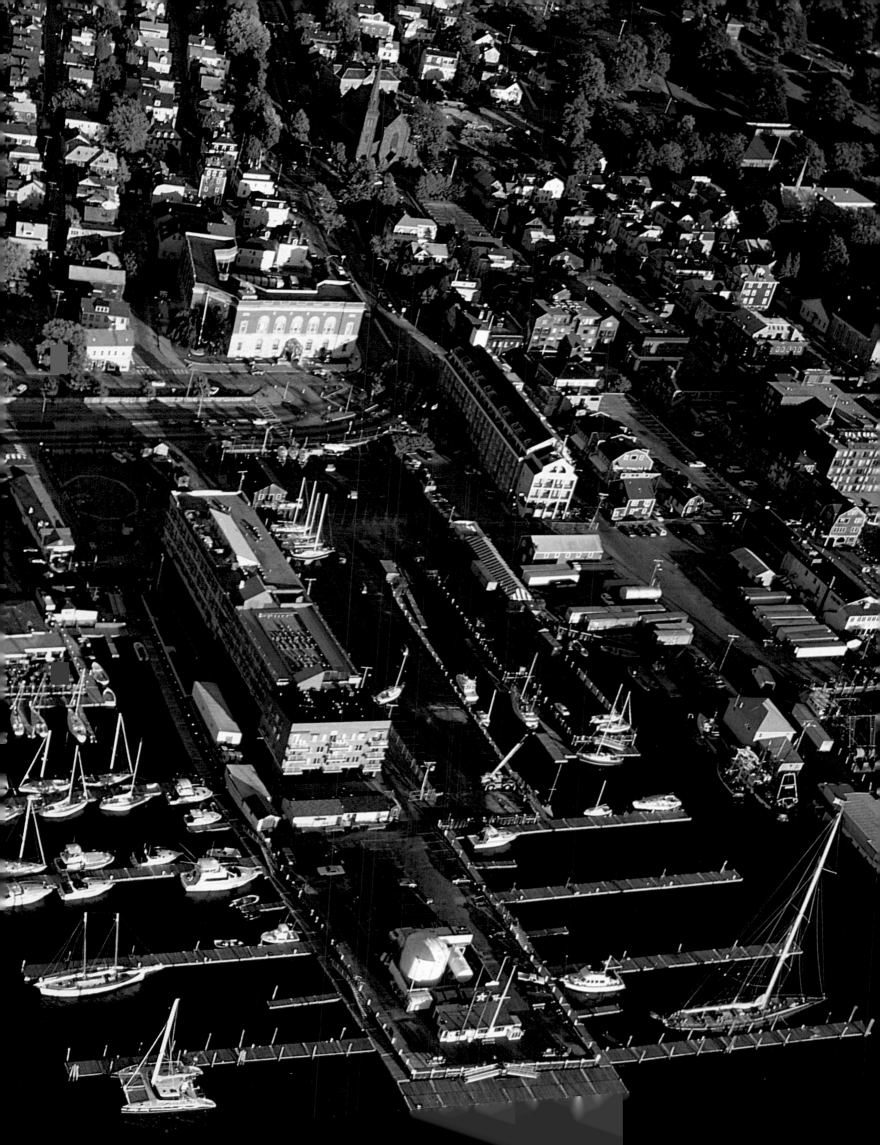

84 top Château-sur-mer is an example of superb Victorian architecture in an American setting. The mansion was built in 1852 for William Wetmore, who had amassed a fortune trading with China. In 1872 it was restructured by the architect R.M. Hunt, one of the first Americans to have studied at the Ecole des Beaux Arts in Paris.

84 bottom and 84-85 The millionaire mansions of Newport are concentrated on the southern tip of Aquidneck Island, fronting the Atlantic Ocean. Anyone wishing to take a closer look at these "cottages" has a choice of routes. Perhaps the most scenic, but also the most physically challenging, is the 3-mile Cliff Walk, a narrow trail which follows Newport's cliffs.

85 Practically all the most opulent residences of Newport are on Bellevue Avenue. This elegant, wide road, which starts downtown, offers fine front views of the properties which, architecturally, have more in common with castles and Renaissance palaces than with mere houses. Their owners brought architects and craftsmen all the way from Europe to contribute to their construction.

86-87 Historic Colonial Newport centres on Washington Square. With its centuries-old Brick Market and well-preserved 18th and 19th century houses, this is the hub of tourist life in the city. The building pictured here is the Court House.

86 top and 87 top Since the demise of its Gilded Age, Newport has been taken over by a new up-and-thriving class. Alongside the old mansions, now open to the public like stately homes, are new houses testifying to the more vibrant and elitist style of the current jetset. In the American press present-day Newport has been called the "new preppie city of the West Coast", a description that fits it perfectly.

87 centre Belcourt Castle, on Bellevue Avenue, was built in 1891 for Oliver Hazard Perry Belmont, heir of the Rothschild fortune; designed in Louis XIII style, it has no fewer than 60 rooms. Belmont married Alva, a socialite of great class and European taste, divorcee of William K. Vanderbilt who owned nearby Marble House. Belcourt Castle later became the residence of the Tinney family, who lived there for over forty years.

87 bottom Tennis, as well as sailing, was one of the favourite sports practised by the beau monde of Gilded Age Newport. America's first national tennis championships were held at the city's Tennis Hall of Fame in 1881. Many important lawn tennis events still take place here but the Tennis Hall of Fame is now best known for a well-endowed museum dedicated to the history of this sport.

88-89 Newport Bridge — connecting Newport to Jamestown and the west side of Rhode Island — is a prominent feature of Narragansett Bay. Newport owes its fortune partly to easy road access and an enviable position: it is only 70 miles from Boston and 165 from New York.

90 Like all the rooms of The Breakers, the dining room is richly decorated: alabaster pillars, frescoed walls, tapestries, mosaics and gilt stuccowork set the stage for diamond-studded parties organized to entertain Newport's summer residents.

92-93 The attractions of Fort Adams State Park, which covers an area of 132 acres, include Fort Adams, built in 1824, and the Museum of Yachting. The fort affords a splendid view over the whole of Narragansett Bay (looking west) and the entrance to Newport Harbor (to the east).

94-95 Newport used to be the scene of the America's Cup, the most important international sailing trophy (and challenge competition), first offered and won in 1851. It moved to Newport in 1930 and remained there without interruption until 1983 when the Australians succeeded in taking the famous trophy from the United States. Pictured here is the Italian yacht Azzurra, during the 1983 America's Cup.

THE NATURE

New England is a territory created by erosion over a period of many thousands of years: ice, wind and water were the fundamental elements that shaped this splendid landscape and left it strewn with rivers and dotted with countless lakes. More than eighty percent of the state is today covered by woods, and in summertime the place is a verdant paradise. But as the end of September approaches nature performs a miracle, turning the landscape into a riot of colour. With the arrival of the Indian Summer, lasting well into November, practically every leaf on every tree is touched by red, orange and gold. It is a moment of pure magic, when the countryside of New England is decked in the bold colours normally admired only in surrealistic

paintings. In terms of spectacle, Vermont takes the prize: three-quarters of this state is wooded and in autumn larch, oak, poplar and birch are ablaze with the warmest tones of the colour spectrum. Should you wish to witness the spectacle at its most stirring moment or simply to be kept in the picture, there is even a telephone service offering progress reports, with daily updated accounts on the yellowing of the foliage; special news bulletins for leaf-watchers are also broadcast over radio. The arrival of winter also turns this landscape into an unforgettable sight: the vast expanses of forest, clad in a dazzlingly white coat of snow, are seemingly dormant or caught in the grips of some mysterious spell that has worked a crystalline metamorphosis. With its vast forests, monuments dedicated to horses and commemorative plaques to felled trees, Vermont is America's most environment-friendly state. So what if it has no seaboard? Does it need one when it has Lake Champlain which, with a surface covering 490 square miles, is the sixth largest lake in the USA? Travelling the length and breadth of Vermont you sense the full wonder of its natural beauty (and an excellent road for this purpose is the winding and often splendidly scenic Route 100): mountains encompassed by

96 Franconia Notch in New Hampshire is an 8-mile pass between the Kinsman and Franconia ranges. Several mountains in this area are named after American presidents, and form the so-called Presidential Range. Among the scenic splendours of Franconia Notch State Park is the Flume. This natural chasm, with narrow granite walls soaring to heights of 60 to 90 feet, is the site of Avalanche Falls. Pictured in this photo are the mirror-like waters of Echo Lake.

97 The scenery of Vermont, one of the smallest states in America, must still look much as it did when the first settlers arrived here: streams with crystal-clear water and vast woods of larch, birch and maple trees which explode into colour as fall approaches. The farmhouse pictured here is in the hamlet of Barnet, one of six villages (the others are Peacham, Groton, Walden, Cabot and Painfield) that form the 'Northeast Kingdom', an area of Vermont particularly known for its rural charm.

98 top This is Orwell, a quiet hamlet on the shores of Lake Champlain in west Vermont. From September to mid-October, on the trails and around the villages scattered about the Green Mountains, far from the milling crowds of towns and cities, nature dons her finery. And tourists come in their thousands to gaze in wonder at the breathtaking riot of colours that accompanies Indian summers.

98-99 The 34-mile Kancamagus Highway, completed only in 1959 (it was started in 1837...), winds its way from Lincoln as far as the Saco River in Conway (New Hampshire). It crosses the White Mountain National Forest, habitat of black bear, moose and lynx which hide among its birch, maple and pine trees. The fiery shades of fall foliage turn the "Kank" into one of the most colourful roads in New England.

wooded slopes, tiny lakes nestling in green valleys, streams of crystal-clear water, pastures dotted with cows and sheep, snug farmsteads that conjure up a world of rustic tranquillity, delightful little bridges reminiscent of Monet paintings... A picturesque scenario that offers so much to discover and enjoy, including the produce of this nature-blessed land. Particularly good buys in the grocery stores of Vermont are the highly rated local Cheddar cheese and maple syrup, used more than sugar around these parts, poured over breakfast pancakes or as a scrumptious topping for vanilla ice cream. Sap is collected from maple trees in many areas of the state: tubing carries the sap from a taphole in the tree to a pan where the liquid is subsequently evaporated to obtain the syrup. In terms of natural environment Maine has a totally different character: here you must listen to the voice of nature. Visitors to Acadia National Park, for example, must stop a while to hear the roar of the Atlantic and to feel the full force of its waves as they rush into Thunder Hole, a natural rocky cave encountered along Ocean Drive. The park, with its 17,000 hectares of unspoilt territory, extends from Mount Desert Island to Isle au Haut, a subartic region which boasts some 500 different species of flowers and over 300 species of birds. An excellent way to get familiar with this unspoiled corner of the state is to abandon motorized transport in favour of something more unconventional: the park can be toured along 35 miles of carriage roads, on a bike, on horseback or in horsedrawn carriages. The route passes some of its most outstanding natural attractions: Cadillac Mountain, only 1,450 feet high but well worth the hike to the top just for the unique panorama; Otter Cliffs, huge slabs of pink granite with a sheer 33-metre drop to the ocean below; Sand Beach, one of the finest along the entire coastline; the deep, deep blue waters of Eagle Lake. For hikers Acadia offers almost 130 miles of paths and trails across woods and mountains and, for anyone physically up to the challenge, lakes and their surroundings can be explored in kayaks and canoes. In Maine another oasis of

100-101 Providence, capital of Rhode Island, is one of the three biggest cities of New England. Tolerance and respect for freethinkers have been cornerstones of the city's ethics since its foundation and are symbolized by the gilded statue "The Independent Man" which tops the huge dome of the State House (second only to St. Peter's in Rome). This imposing building, constructed in 1900 from white Georgian marble, is situated on Constitution Hill, one of the three hills on which Providence stands; the other two are College Hill and Federal Hill.

100 top and 101 top Providence was founded in 1636 by Roger Williams on the river of the same name, formed by the confluence of the rivers Mohassuck and Woonasquatucket. In East Providence, Benefit Road — known as the "Mile of History" — has many 18th century buildings of red brick with white marble trim. Pictured in these photos are Crowford Street Bridge with the Courthouse (left), and Providence River (right).

peace and quiet where nature reigns supreme is to be found in Baxter Park, habitat of moose and of the common loon, in the heart of the North Woods. The flow of tourists into the park is strictly controlled according to accommodation available in its campsite. With the hundreds of lakes and ponds dotted about this huge wilderness, the only way to get around is by canoe or on foot. The whole area was purchased by Percival Baxter, a rich governor of Maine: he used his very substantial resources to acquire ownership — bit by bit — of the unspoiled woods, lakes and streams that encompass Katahdin, the state's highest mountain. His objective was to save this preserve of nature from the voracious appetite of the paper industry. Before his death Baxter bequeathed it all to the nation, entrusting its protection to the state. For water and snow sports aficionados, New Hampshire has the highest mountains in the northeastern United States and is undoubtedly an idyllic destination. As their name suggests, the White Mountains are snow-capped practically all year round. Presiding over the landscape is Mount Washington, which soars to a height of 6,280 metres. The state boasts 1,300 lakes and ponds, each with its own special beauty and appeal, and it's not surprising that — besides skiing — the most popular sporting activity around these parts is canoeing. Descending rivers in kayaks can be another thrilling experience. In Rhode Island rolling farmland stretches as far as the horizon, the terrain crisscrossed by picturesque country roads and paths that appear to have been put there with bikers in mind. In spite of its diminutive size, this state too has plentiful evidence of generosity on the part of Mother Nature, who left many gems here. And the long-entrenched ecological conscience of the local people has ensured these irreplaceable assets remain unharmed: protected areas have been created here, for instance, the Wickaboxet forest or the Emile Ruecker nature reserve, originally a private estate, where over 100 different species of birds nest and breed. Considered most typical of Massachusetts is the Berkshires region, which occupies its

102 top Yale has no fewer
than two hundred buildings:
some of them — like
Harkness Tower, seen here —
are examples of traditional
Gothic architecture, others
are ultra-modern.

102 bottom and 102-103 The
Green — a 16-acre plot in the
centre of New Haven,
Connecticut — has been the
focal point of city life since it
was set aside as a town
common by the earliest
settlers in 1638. The Country
Courthouse, opposite the
Green in Elm Street, is just
one of the many public
buildings that sprung up
around it.

western end. Many rivers and streams flow through this
more hilly than mountainous area. Marking its border are
the Taconic and Hoosac mountains, regarded as
impenetrable until the 18th century: the only way to cross
them was along the Mohawk Trail left by native Americans
(and now the main route taken by anyone heading for the
Great Lakes). This verdant setting is a popular choice for the
holiday homes of New Yorkers and Bostonians, who
appreciate the leisurely pace and caring spirit that still
feature large in the life of its tiny village communities.
The serene atmosphere that pervades Massachusetts is not
without a romantic element, which explains the special
appeal of this state to many great American writers of the
19th century who made it their home and inspiration.
West of Boston, the town of Concord evokes stories of
touching romanticism: still standing here is the timber-built
house where Louisa May Alcott wrote "Little Women".
Within its walls time seems to have stood still and one
almost expects the March girls to come bursting onto the
scene. Massachusetts has a distinctive flavour all of its own:
the taste of cranberries. The crops harvested in the state meet
half the demand of the American market.

From end of September to early November the area around
the small town of Carver, a short distance from Cape Cod, is
transformed into bogs, known to local folk as "the land of a
thousand lakes": the fields where cranberries are growing
are flooded so that the ruby-red berries float and harvesting
is made easier. And what delights of nature are revealed in
Boston? Of course, there is Boston Common, the oldest
public park in the United States.
But the city also has the "hidden gardens" of Beacon Hill,
the old Puritan district of Boston.
Rain or shine, each year on the third Wednesday in May, the
wood and wrought-iron gates of these private gardens are
opened, offering a unique chance to walk down narrow
paths bordered by thick hedges of ivy and jasmine, and to
admire the intricate floral designs that embellish these
treasured places.

103 top Depicted in this photo is Memorial Hall, part of Yale University. This seat of learning was founded in 1701 thanks to Elihu Yale, a wealthy merchant and official of the East India Company. With Havard, the university is one of America's oldest and most famous campuses.

104 top The Peabody and Essex Museum houses — in its thirty rooms — thousands of artifacts imported from Asia and the Pacific when the East Indies Maritime Company had its warehouse in Salem. The Peabody Museum also has a collection of old nautical instruments, maps, logbooks and figure-heads that once embellished the bows of sailing vessels.

104-105 The name of Salem, in Massachusetts, brings to mind the witch trials held here in 1692. But above all Salem was a flourishing centre of maritime trade. The Derby House (shown in the photo), a Georgian residence of 1762, with its authentic 18th furnishings, was the home of Elias Hasket Derby, the wealthiest man in Salem's history.

105 top and centre The House of the Seven Gables also owes its fame to a novel by Hawthorne. Built in 1668 — before the witchcraft trials — for John Turner, a ship's captain, this gloomy mansion is one of the oldest surviving buildings in New England and its interior still conveys the austere atmosphere typical of 17th century Puritan households. It has a mysterious secret staircase, thought to have been used by fleeing black slaves brought here from the Caribbean.

105 bottom Salem Maritime is a National Historic Site, comprising 17th and 18th century wharves and harbour buildings like the Bonded Warehouse and the West India Store. Tours also take in the Custom House, a building in classical style with a golden eagle (symbol of America) decorating its façade. In 1846 Nathaniel Hawthorne, celebrated author of "The Scarlet Letter", worked here as port surveyor.

106-107 The Berkshire Hills have a special charm which has long attracted writers and artists. Herman Melville wrote "Moby Dick" in his home in Arrowhead, near Pittsfield, and at The Mount — a house she herself designed and had built near Lenox — Edith Wharton penned "The Age of Innocence".

108-109 Franconia Notch, Profile Lake, the Old Man of the Mountains and Cannon Mountain — a natural rock formation resembling a cannon — are some of the many scenic features of the White Mountains region, with its spectacular peaks.

108 top and 109 top The Monadnock region, in the south-west of New Hampshire, has thirty-nine hamlets, villages and towns, each offering its own distinctive interpretation of Old England style. Rising high above them is Grand Monadnock, reputedly one of the most climbed mountains in America.

109 bottom The granite profile of the Old Man of the Mountains is clearly visible from the shores of glacially carved Profile Lake in Franconia Notch State Park. The giant stone face, considered to resemble President Lincoln, has been around some 20,000 years, inspiring legends and poetry.

110-111 The villages of the Berkshires, nestling in peaceful valleys and encompassed by huge forests and lakes with crystalline waters, were a major source of ideas for Herman Melville. And the massive, snow-capped form of Mt. Greylock apparently inspired him to make Moby Dick.

112 top Just a few miles from Worcester in Massachusetts is Old Sturbridge Village. Founded by Albert and J.C. Wells, this outdoor museum is a working model of a New England village between 1790 and 1840, presenting many facets of everyday life in a rural community. On Sundays leading up to Christmas visitors can join in the fun of Holiday Magic, a show performed in a real party atmosphere.

112 bottom The White Mountains get their name from the thick blanket of snow that changes the face of the region in winter. After falls of snow the landscape comes to life as crowds of skiers pack lift facilities, the cable-car to the top of Cannon Mountain (4,200 feet) and the cog railroad train that creeps up Mount Washington (6,290 feet). Dartmouth Carnival is celebrated in the villages at the foot of these mountains, with hockey matches, downhill and cross-country skiing races, ski acrobatics and ice sculpture competitions.

112-113 Historic Deerfield in Massachusetts — settled in the 1660s and twice plundered by rampaging Indians — still has many old Colonial buildings, among them Frary House (1720), as the inn pictured here was called, and Ashley House (1730). An overview of the town's history is offered by collections of old prints, photographs and period costumes exhibited in the Memorial Hall Museum; the most interesting item displayed is undoubtedly the door of John Sheldon House, bearing clear signs of the Indian attack of 1704. The unreal atmosphere of Deerfield is heightened in winter, when it becomes difficult to tell the preserved "museum-buildings" from the private homes all around.

113 top Martha's Vineyard is just a few miles off the coast of Cape Cod. Upscale architecture and laid-back lifestyle have made the island fashionable with the rich and famous. A favourite site is Oak Bluffs, with its numerous, gaily painted Victorian "gingerbread cottages", seemingly straight out of a fairy tale. In winter a coat of soft white snow creates an atmosphere of unbelievable peace and beauty.

114 top A few miles from Burlington, Vermont, picturesquely situated on the shores of Lake Champlain, is the Shelburne Museum. Standing on a 45-acre property once owned by the family of Dr. Seward Webb, it is comprised of 35 buildings, all open to the public: some are reconstructions, others are authentic period buildings, such as the Queen Ann Revival House, with 110 rooms, and Shelburne House (in the photo), an old inn with 29 bedrooms.

114 bottom Electra, Dr. Webb's daughter, inherited her father's love of art and gradually put together a vast collection of Americana, including artifacts, jewellery, Indian craft products, even a steamship and a railroad locomotive. The collection now belongs to the Shelburne Museum. Pictured here is the General Store.

114-115 Once Iroquois Indian hunting territory, then a French and later English colony, Vermont remains close to its traditions. Considered the Switzerland of North America, this state has an essentially agricultural economy. A large percentage of its population still live in rural communities and work on the land.

115 top Halloween is celebrated on October 31 throughout the USA but it is attributed particular importance down the East Coast. Children in fancy dress gather together to go knocking on doors, asking for cookies and little gifts. Pumpkins emptied of their flesh and carved into huge, grinning faces are used as lanterns or for making grotesque masks and puppets.

115 bottom Peacham, in the so-called Northeast Kingdom, is one of the most photographed villages in Vermont: with its white timber houses, church with pointed steeple, apple trees and carpet of colourful foliage, it certainly presents a pretty picture.

116 Lake Willoughby is also situated in the Northeast Kingdom. Vermont's lack of an Atlantic seaboard is amply compensated by the many lakes, rivers and streams hidden deep in its forests or crossed by covered bridges, creating countless stunning landscapes.

116-117 Lake Champlain stretches for 120 miles, from New York State to the Canadian border. Its widest point — 12 miles — is by the city of Burlington. On the waters of this lake, the sixth largest in the nation, anglers catch plentiful pickerel, perch and bass and boating enthusiasts can set sail for one of the three islands to the north: Isle La Motte, North Hero and Grand Island.

117 top In Plymouth county, Cape Cod and on the islands of Martha's Vineyard and Nantucket, cranberries are harvested in September and October. Fields are flooded to make it easier to gather in the crop, ready to be turned into juice, jellies, jam and wine. Villages and towns in these areas organize their own Cranberry Harvest Festival and the celebrations attract visitors by the thousands.

118-119 In the countryside of Vermont isolated farmsteads with red barns and shiny silos are not an unusual sight. Here time seems to have stood still: products like maple syrup, cheddar cheese and apple wines still occupy an important place among Vermonters'"exports". And when it comes to their homes, furniture and work tools, they still like to practise the age-old art of "doing it themselves".

121 In fall colour becomes the keynote of a magical landscape. And from early September to mid-October the whole of New England participates in this colourful pageant. This photograph was taken at Crawford Notch, close to Arethusa Falls.

120 The blazing colours of fall are worthy of a surrealist painting. In the woods and forests of New England the gleaming gold and burning red of maple, larch, birch and oak turn the landscape into a stunningly colourful sight. The Mohawk Trail in Massachusetts offers breathtaking panoramas. In the foliage season the trees change hue again and again before finally shedding their leaves. This spectacle of nature has enormous appeal for tourists who, like the pioneers of the past, venture down trails and along rivers in search of the most rapturous sights. Leaf-watchers can even call a Fall Foliage Hotline for information, and the radio also broadcasts a daily bulletin, with suggested itineraries.

122 top Close to a New England farmstead stands a typical red-painted timber barn, with a huge maple tree in the foreground. These trees sometimes grow to a enormous height and a tree's leaf can be of different colours, ranging from red to yellow. The syrup obtained from them has to be boiled again and again in special pans before it is poured into jars, ready for consumption. Americans are passionately fond of maple syrup, especially spread on their breakfast pancakes.

122 bottom Kinsman Notch is a pass between the valleys of the Connecticut and Pemigewasset rivers, a few miles from the village of Lincoln. People come here to see the glacially formed gorge of the Lost River, which has carved tortuous ravines and caves along its course.

123 top This huge stone barn breaks away from traditional designs for agricultural buildings, as do other structures at Shelburne Farms. With the aid of landscape architect Frederick Law Olmsted, Dr. W. Seward Webb introduced experimental farming methods here.

123 bottom The covered bridges that occasionally cross New England's rivers and streams offer a romantic and nostalgic picture of Old America. The bridge in this photo is located in New Hampshire.

124-125 As its name suggests, the Mohawk Trail, in Massachusetts, was once used by Indians. Widened by settlers, it later became one of the most famous scenic routes in America. Along its 63 miles, from Orange to Williamstown, the road passes through some of the loveliest places in New England.

126-127 Extending to the borders with New Hampshire and Canada, Vermont's Northeast Kingdom is generously endowed with forests, lakes, valleys and picturesque mountain villages. Not far from the Burkes villages — East Burke, Burke Hollow and West Burke — is Lake Willoughby, with the surrounding cliffs of Mount Pisgah reflected in its waters.

128 Along the Freedom Trail, the Old State House was the first public building in Boston, erected in 1713. The lion and unicorn on its façade are symbols of the British Crown; they are copies of the original ones destroyed by fire on July 4, 1776, date of the Declaration of Independence which was read for the first time on this very spot. The Old State House is now a museum with collections tracing Boston's history.

NEW ENGLAND

CONTENTS